Wild Hoofbeats

AMERICA'S VANISHING WILD HORSES

BY CAROL WALKER

FOREWORD BY GINGER KATHRENS

FOREWORD

BY GINGER KATHRENS

When a nearly white, newborn wild horse foal tottered out of the trees right in front of my camera in 1995, I thought how "lucky" I was. Years later I realized that the encounter with the colt I named Cloud had altered the course of my life. It has become my mission to try to preserve not only Cloud and his family, but also his herd, and other wild horse herds still remaining in the west.

Carol Walker also fell under the powerful spell that wild horses cast. Her encounter with a gray stallion on a cold April morning in southern Wyoming changed her life too. And how lucky we are that these two met, for it allows us to see mustangs through the eyes of a gifted photographer. Carol's striking images grace nearly every page of this handsome and artistic work. Her personal stories of the wild horses she came to know and love reveal her deep understanding of what makes a wild horse tick—a love of family and freedom.

Carol also reveals how their complex society works and how easily it is shattered during government round ups. It may have taken a stallion a lifetime to build a family, only to lose everything in an instant. Mares and their stallions are ripped apart, their offspring taken away from them. It is a violent and heartbreaking event. I have experienced it and so has Carol. She describes so poignantly the cruelty and callousness of what she has seen firsthand.

In *Wild Hoofbeats*, Carol courageously tells of the threats to the wild horses clinging to their freedom on our public lands in the west. Though beloved by the public, they are largely reviled by extractive users of these lands. Why? The few thousand mustangs compete with millions of head of cattle and sheep for grass. And the blame for any damage to the land is conveniently attributed to wild horses. The government's solution to the "problem" is to remove the mustangs–not the cattle and sheep. There are currently more unadopted mustangs imprisoned in pens, pastures, and corrals than roaming free on the range.

Another successful tactic public lands ranchers use (with the support of the Bureau of Land Management) is to claim that mustangs are starving and must be removed. Look carefully at Carol's pictures taken in all seasons in Adobe Town. Do these look like the starving mustangs? This myth is as outrageous as the claim they are over populated and are eating themselves out of house and home. Of course, millions of cattle graze the ranges, but they are not the problem?

Now another threat looms on the wide western horizon, one that is much scarier than millions of cows. Oil and gas exploration is exploding on public lands, the very lands where we still find mustangs. It threatens to squeeze the few remaining herds into oblivion.

Yet, the American public can do something to avoid the extinction of the wild horse. Their voices were heard in 1971 and Congress unanimously voted to save them. We need to again rally behind our spectacular, embattled mustangs and the wild lands they roam.

These are America's wild horses. They belong to the American public and they deserve to live forever free with their families in wide open spaces that still boggle the imagination–places like Adobe Town in southern Wyoming… a place that Carol Walker knows well.

Flint, after Cloud kicks him out of the band, is finally a bachelor stallion at 5 years old.

INTRODUCTION

In the distance, dust boils up off the prairie. In a land that seems empty of all but sagebrush, wisps of grass, dirt and sun, the sight is riveting. As the dust rises slowly, moving shapes begin to take form: white blazes, flashing eyes, manes flying and tails waving, the occasional sharp hoof. There is sound too, a gradually growing dull thunder that vibrates the ground like an enduring earthquake. Soon dust, shapes, and sounds resolve themselves into running horses–a huge number of running horses. The prairie in the American West must have looked like this when the 19th century turned to the 20th, and millions of wild horses roamed free.

When Congress passed the Wild Free-Roaming Horse and Burro Act in 1971, it declared that wild horses "are living symbols of the historic and pioneer spirit of the West; that they contribute to the diversity of life forms within the Nation and en-rich the lives of the American people," and that "they are fast disappearing from the Western Landscape." As such, Congress made clear its policy: "that wild free-roaming horses and burros shall be protected from capture, branding, harassment, or death; and to accomplish this they are to be considered in the area where presently found, as an integral part of the natural system of the public lands."

▶ *A young chestnut stallion grazes on a ridge with his small band. Suddenly, an older stallion approaches.*

The chestnut stallion struts up to the intruder, neck arched, nostrils flaring, and paws the ground.

The two stallions sniff noses, and then, intimidated, the older stallion runs away, back the way he came.

Wild horses epitomize the spirit of the Old West, and the romance between man, wildlife, and the land. Icons of the West and the frontier spirit of America, they played an integral part in the evolution of our nation, from the time of the Indians to the first explorers, as the first horses of the cowboy, and as the mounts of the cavalry in World War I. Early white settlers enjoyed the sights of hundreds of thousands of horses boiling across the plains.

Just as Americans coming from another land reveled in new-found space and opportunities, so too did the wild horse come from afar and embrace his freedom in this country. In the course of our nation's history, however, wild horses have been considered resources to be exploited as well as pests to be eliminated. And now the wild horse is on the verge of being removed entirely from our nation's public lands. Only the outcry of America's people can change the fate of the last wild horses.

Wild horses in 10 states have been pushed to the poorest of lands and the harshest of living conditions, yet they have managed to adapt and thrive. Ten western states (Arizona, California, Colorado, Idaho, Montana, Nevada, New Mexico, Oregon, Utah, and Wyoming) have populations of horses managed by the Bureau of Land Management (BLM), more than half of which are in the State of Nevada. The state with the second largest number of wild horses is Wyoming, with over 3300 wild horses in 16 Herd Management Areas.

The chestnut stallion gallops to rejoin his band. ◀

THE AD

OBE TOWN WILD HORSE HERD

The largest wild horse herd in Wyoming, in fact one of the last large herds in the United States, roams the BLM's Adobe Town Herd Management Area, which lies in the southwestern corner of the state. Adobe Town is in the Red Desert, a remote and vast landscape with astounding dramatic red and pink buttes, rolling and dusty sands, and canyons whose rock strata speak of geologic eras rather than years. The Herd Management Area consists of over 450,000 acres, with sagebrush, sparse grass, and an average rainfall of only 7 inches a year. Even though it is a brutal, lonely, and unforgiving landscape, the wild horses of the Adobe Town Herd thrive there.

Over a 4-year period, I followed and photographed horses from seven of the bands that make up the Adobe Town herd, through summer and winter, during high winds, driving rain, and freezing cold. I witnessed newborn foals, violent challenges between the stallions, tender moments between mares and foals–and between yearlings and stallions–and peaceful moments at rest. At the end, I had to say a final goodbye to over half the members of the herd as they were rounded up and removed from the area–and from their freedom.

16

During my visits to the Adobe Town Herd, the sight of another human was rare, even though rutted roads wind their way through the area, with the newer ones leading to recent oil drilling sites. The occasional white pickups that passed me belonged to the oil company workers, who most days traveled fast enough to generate a lot of dust or, during a rare wet period, to leave deep furrows in the mud for me to negotiate later. But as a rule, the oil workers don't usually stop to watch the horses, and probably never get out of their vehicles to walk out in the sagebrush to take a closer look. Like many people in this country, the oil workers take the horses–true emblems of the West–for granted.

In wild horse society, a band is a close social group that lives together, protected by a stallion, who brings up the rear when the herd travels and stands watch while the others graze and rest. The band is often led by an older, experienced mare, the "lead mare," who is alert to threats and knows the optimum routes to the best places for water, shelter, and forage. Wild horses may have a range as large as 10 miles. They have a general area where they graze and identify water holes spaced many miles apart that they may travel to within a day.

In the Adobe Town Herd, the bands are small, with groups ranging from two to seven horses. Family is all important to wild horses. The stallions will fight off other stallions and intruders to jealously guard their bands. As the foals are born, the mares come into "foal heat," making them receptive to the stallions and ready to be bred (although the mares do not necessarily conceive when bred in this first heat after foaling). Because many of these mares come into season at the same time during the foaling season, during this period the stallions are aggressive and possessive of their own mares and even attempt to steal mares from other stallions.

18

191

Rock Springs

I-80

To Rawlins ->

789

Salt Wells Creek

191

Adobe Town

WYOMING

UTAH

COLORADO

N

0 3 6   12   18   24
Miles

▶ *At left shows the Adobe Town and Salt Wells Herd Management areas in southwestern Wyoming.*

At right shows the wild horse herd management areas in Wyoming.

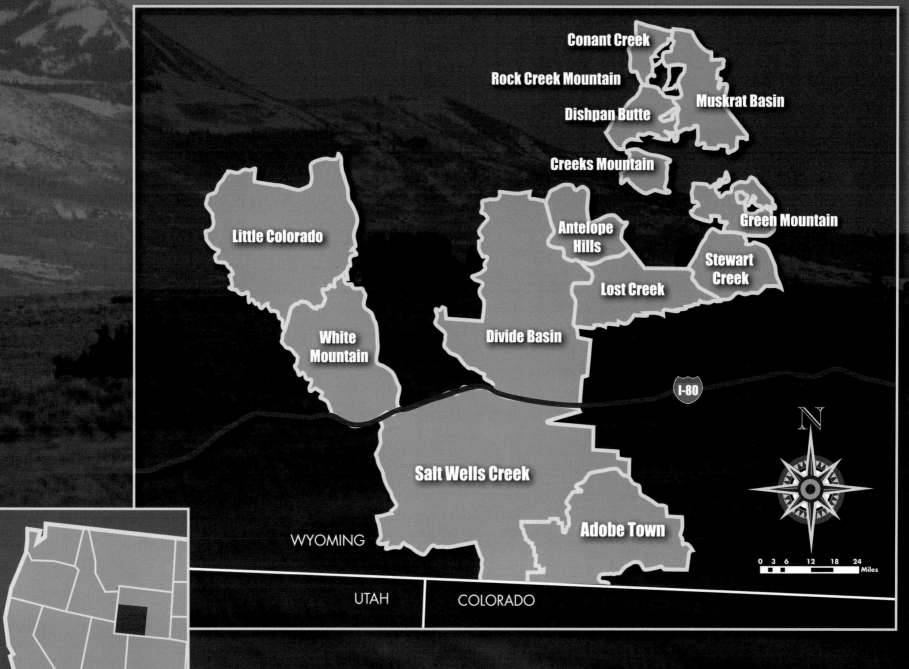

HERD MANAGEMENT AREAS

SOUTH WYOMING

Conant Creek

Rock Creek Mountain

Dishpan Butte

Muskrat Basin

Creeks Mountain

Little Colorado

Green Mountain

Antelope Hills

Stewart Creek

Lost Creek

White Mountain

Divide Basin

I-80

Salt Wells Creek

Adobe Town

WYOMING

UTAH   COLORADO

N

0 3 6   12   18   24
Miles

Foals are born in the spring and early summer, and usually remain with the band until they are 2 or 3 years old. The fillies leave when they first go into estrous, and the stallions usually drive off the young colts when they are about 3 years old, not wanting to leave a possible rival in their own band. Since horses are social animals and don't want to be alone, the young stallions will sometimes form "bachelor bands."

Some bands will stay in close proximity to another band, and it seems as though the stallions of these neighboring bands have respect for each other, not trying to steal each other's mares, but occasionally meeting to "greet" each other, with arched necks, pawing, and a sharp squeal or two. They usually part amicably and return to their respective bands. However, few sights can equal the majestic beauty of a wild stallion trumpeting a challenge and then defending his band from a rival.

In the spring as the mares drop their foals and come into season, blood runs hot and competition for mares is fierce. Ears pricked forward, nostrils flaring and muscles trembling, the stallion will rush toward the intruder and stop a few feet away. The stallions sniff each other with necks arched so tightly it seems painful. Suddenly, one stallion paws first the ground, then the air, in an aggressive dance with his opponent. Necks scarred with the history of other challenges, the stallions rear and strike at each other, until the less dominant stallion comes down from his hind legs and gallops away back to his band. As he approaches his mares, the stallion lowers and twists his head in a motion aptly called "snaking," and then he drives his mares and foals to a safe distance. Dust flies up as the band, with long, tangled manes waving and tails brushing the earth, continues to run, not in flight, but for the sheer joy of being alive and free.

The colors of the wild horses in Adobe Town are predominantly gray, with red and blue roans, some blacks, and few bays and chestnuts. Standing at average heights of about 15 hands and weighing about 1000 pounds, the horses in this area are larger than in many of the wild horse herds in other parts of the country. In the summer, their coats are slick and healthy, and in the winter the hair coats thicken as luxuriously as ermine or mink.

Winter can be a cruel time in Adobe Town. During one of my visits, the wind-driven chill penetrated my thickest parka and stunned me with its viciousness. In early March, winter had not yet loosened its grip on the high desert. Although it was dry, there were dabs of snow on the tops of mesas, and most of the vegetation was still brown. But the horses were better equipped than I was. They had their winter protection–long, fuzzy hair that made even that year's foals resemble woolly stuffed animals. As cold as the winters do generally become, with driving wind and tempera-tures sometimes below zero, the horses manage to thrive and find food.

The first Adobe Town band to capture my imagination belonged to a light-gray stallion. I remember our meeting vividly.

The sorrel stallion comes close

to investigate in the soft light of dawn

Winter brings snow and freezing winds to the herd area, and the horses struggle to survive.

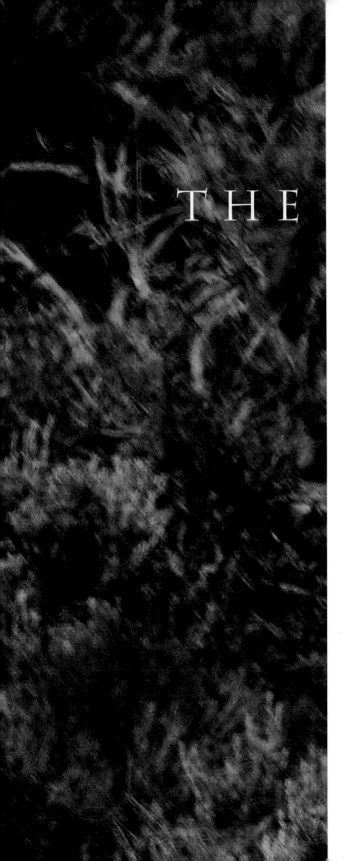

THE GRAY STALLION

It is late April, the morning of my first day looking for horses in Adobe Town. I have been searching the landscape for sight of the herd, but so far even my binoculars have shown me nothing except endless acres of sage and pale soil, tossed up into mocking dust devils by the spring wind. I force my car over deep ruts, wrench the steering to round a bend in the primitive road—and spot a graceful white mare, standing 75 feet from the car. Her eyes are closed as she sleeps on her feet, and, below her, ears are sticking out from the sagebrush. A band of wild horses is lying down, sheltering from the bitter wind that seems to blow continuously in this area.

I grab my camera and button my coat, my fingers fumbling with the buttons as I rush. When I get out of the car, I leave the door ajar to avoid making unnecessary noise. I ease toward the horses. Abruptly, a light-gray horse with a charcoal mane lunges to its feet and begins running toward me. I realize that this must be the stallion. As he gets closer and closer, I wonder if he is going to stop. I also wonder what I will do if he doesn't. As he approaches, more horses behind him unfold their bodies and rise up from the sagebrush. I see two fillies, one a gawky yearling and the other, a sturdier 2-year-old. I am a statue.

The stallion slows to a trot and then stops about 10 feet away from me, and I finally breathe, thrilled to see him so close. He is downwind, so he can smell me. He seems to be inspecting me as avidly as I am him. From the many bite marks and scars sprinkled across his white coat, he is clearly an older stallion. Once he has taken a good look, he seems to relax and strolls over to the younger of the two fillies, which are standing together looking at me. The two sisters look alike, with similar straight blazes on their faces, but the smaller filly's blaze tapers between her eyes like an hourglass. She is a reddish color but is turning gray like her mother and father. The stallion stops beside her and affectionately nuzzles her, and she nuzzles him back. Then he walks over to the larger filly, a rosy pink, and nuzzles her. She lifts her head, showing her teeth as though she were grinning at me. I laugh, and, luckily, the horses don't seem to care after all about the noise I make.

The mare hangs back, watching her daughters' antics. Her belly is very large with this year's coming foal. Not wanting to interfere in their morning activities, I leave when the horses start becoming restless.

▶ *The white mare's belly*

seems huge the night

before she foals

A month later, I again find the light-gray stallion, who is amply decorated now with battle scars, and his band, which still includes the all-white mare and two graying fillies. They are down below a huge butte, sheltered from the wind. It is too steep for me to climb down and approach closer, so I watch from above. It is getting late in the day, time to head back to town. I notice that the heavily pregnant mare looks ready to give birth very soon.

The next morning, I drive to the same area and get out of my vehicle. I am hopeful that I will see the same band again. When I see a flash of white from behind a rise, I start walking cautiously toward the band. The mare and her two fillies are lying down, and, nestled by the mare's side, is a new colt, only hours old, with a jagged blaze down his brown face. The stallion starts toward me, comes downwind, then stops and puts his head down to graze, untroubled by my careful, slow approach.

I sit down about 25 feet from the band to observe and take pictures. It is a peaceful scene: The foal is avidly nursing, and the fillies continue to doze. Suddenly, a high-pitched squeal erupts from the other side of the rise. But the light-gray stallion seems unconcerned, clearly a veteran of many such challenges.

Then six horses, all dark gray, lope over the rise, stop at the sight of the light-gray stallion's band, and begin scuffling with each other. It is not clear who is in charge within the new arrivals, as a stout dappled mare squeals and strikes at a young stallion, which makes only a half-hearted attempt to argue back. All of the dark grays seem skittish and insecure, perhaps because they have no real leader. As this unruly group approaches, the white mare, her fillies, and the foal get up and start walking away while the light-gray stallion stands with every sense alert, waiting to see what will happen. When the interlopers get too close, he rushes over the hill toward them, and a young, dark-gray stallion runs to meet him. They both rear up, striking at each other. They never connect, and the younger stallion, intimidated, gallops away, with his band whinnying and squealing around him. The light-gray stallion and his band amble slowly on down the canyon, with the foal close to his mother's side, keeping up amazingly well for a youngster only a few hours old.

▶ *The young band of intruders disturbs the gray stallion and his newborn foal*

43

The gray stallion runs to protect his band

A month later, through my binoculars I spot the same light-gray stallion about a quarter of a mile from the road on the crest of a hill. I park my vehicle, and, camera in hand, I start hiking toward them. When I am still a long way off and as I am carefully picking a path through the sagebrush, the stallion spots me and runs toward me to investigate. He moves downwind, stops about 20 feet away, puts his head down, licking and chewing, and then turns to head back to his band, as if to tell the others, "Oh, it's just her." I follow him slowly up the hill and sit down about 25 feet away, which seems to be the closest distance that is comfortable for the band. I notice that the older, lighter colored filly, the 2-year-old, is missing. I had heard that when young mares reach the age to breed, they will leave their bands, thus providing a natural deterrent to inbreeding.

It is nap time for the foal, which folds its legs and collapses right in front of his mother. Then the yearling filly lies down in front of the stallion, whose eyes are closed. The mare arranges herself carefully on the ground next to her foal, and, finally, the stallion lies down as well. As I sit there quietly watching–with the ever-present wind blowing, the horses sleeping, deep stillness in sagebrush and sky, and no one else around for miles–I feel blessed to be with these wild horses.

Soon the stallion gets to his feet and walks over to the colt, which is still sleeping, although his mother is now up and eating the sparse grass. The stallion starts nibbling on the colt's mane, and the colt starts protesting, whinnying to his mother, who keeps grazing. The stallion begins grazing, and the colt falls back asleep.

In July, the air is still and hot, and the flies are tormenting the horses even worse than they bother me. I drive along the stretches of uneven and dented road where I saw the light-gray stallion's band before, but so far, I do not see them. It is midmorning, the time of the day that the band likes to nap, and I finally decide to try a new area, which I can reach by a grindstone road that used to be the main road through the area before all the oil drilling brought new and wider roads. This road has fallen into neglect from disuse; it is narrow, has huge potholes, and is broken up by cracks in the earth eroded by flash flooding, so I drive very slowly, looking from side to side while also minding the rapidly changing road surface.

Again, I see a flash of white in the distance, and I pull out my binoculars to get a closer look at two white horses standing together. There is a good chance that this is the light-gray stallion's band. I start a long walk to where I last saw the horses. The grass is rich here, and it is off of the busy main road so it is a popular area for many bands, but the light-gray stallion likes to avoid other bands, so I wonder why he has led his family here. As I get closer, I see the gray stallion taking a dust bath—a good way to protect against the biting flies. The white mare and the yearling filly stand together, and I don't see the little colt. I worry that perhaps he has not made it, then remember that this is the time of the morning that I usually see him napping. As I get closer, I see little ears twitching underneath the white mare. All is well. The mare and filly watch me closely as I approach, but the stallion looks sleepy and unconcerned.

Soon the little colt gets up, and I see that his coat has become much lighter, almost matching his sister's pinkish gray. He stretches his long legs out behind him and then moves over to his sister, who is trying to take a nap. He starts pulling and biting her ears and head, which wakes her up. The stallion moves much closer to me, about 10 feet away, lies down in what must be his favorite dust bath spot, and rolls back and forth. The colt watches curiously. The stallion pauses while still on the ground, makes himself comfortable, and starts lazily grazing on a patch of grass next to him before finally getting to his feet and shaking off the dust. The mare seems restless and starts moving away with the colt and filly close behind, perhaps headed toward the water hole. This is the last time I will see this band.

THE SPANISH STALLION

My first encounter with this gorgeous white stallion comes on a day when I am walking out into a huge meadow that is filled with wild horses divided into bands. It is springtime, which means that it is also foaling time—the period of greatest rivalry between stallions. With only an uneasy truce existing between the bands, scuffles break out from time to time as one band drifts too close to another.

Looking across the huge rolling plain, I can see necks arching, hooves plunging, and the sudden dash of one stallion chasing another away. I wade into the middle of three herds, and none of them are paying much attention to me. Suddenly, I am spotted by an all-white stallion and an older, flea-bitten gray mare, a black yearling, and a chestnut two year old. All four raise their heads and stiffen, then they start trotting up a hillside in front of me. I crouch down, hoping they will approach closer.

The Spanish stallion runs up almost too close, and then lifts his lip to catch my scent in a behavior called flehmen.

The stallion leads. His chiseled head, floating trot, and proud demeanor remind me of the domestic Spanish horses I have seen. He seems young, with not a mark on him from fighting. As they reach the top of the hill, the mare and stallion pause against the blue, blue sky dotted with scudding, puffy clouds. I hold my breath at the dramatic sight. Then the stallion wheels and paws. Even though he is facing the other direction, he remains aware of me. They head down the hill together, and the stallion trots purposefully toward me. I sit still on the ground, and he stops, a gleam of challenge in his eyes. Then he ambles casually away toward his band, which has already begun grazing.

I met up with this stallion and his band almost every time I went to Wyoming to visit the Adobe Town Herd. They are easy to spot, with two gray adults, and they are often near the road. Most of the Adobe Town bands remain in the same general territory: about 5-10 square miles that includes at least one waterhole.

On my next visit, I spot the Spanish stallion and his band in the same meadow. They are grazing near a band I have seen them near before, a band led by a black stallion. I am focused on watching the black stallion from my usual sitting-on-the-ground position when suddenly I hear hoof beats coming rapidly toward me. It is the Spanish stallion, and his white mane and tail are streaming as he runs. He snorts twice and tosses his head, sounding and looking annoyed. I feel very small and very alone as I watch him and wonder if he will stop before he stomps me. My plan is that if he doesn't stop, I will jump to my feet and start screaming and waving my arms above my head to appear larger. Fortunately, just before I am ready to leap into action, he stops so abruptly he kicks up dust. He watches me and snorts again, a harsh burst of air loud in the silence. He appears enormous, all puffed up, and especially huge from my point of view on the ground. Then he lifts his lip at me, and it looks like a gesture of contempt. I start laughing; I cannot help it. This behavior is called "flehmen," and stallions do this to increase their ability to scent mares in heat. Finally, deciding not to adopt me into his band, he strolls away from me to his band.

When I return the following March, I find the Spanish stallion with changes in his band. I wonder what happened and wish they could tell me. The black filly and the chestnut filly are gone; in their place is a motley yearling filly who is in the awkward, patchy stage of turning gray. Her bald face gives her a goofy, inquisitive appearance. The flea-bitten mare remains, but her thick winter coat has turned to a fluffy white, and her large belly hints at the foal to come. The stallion comes trotting quickly toward me, ahead of the mare and filly, and, when he gets close, he snorts at me. As the filly comes closer, curiously examining me, the stallion runs in front of her and the mare as if to warn them not to get too close. After a short time they move off to graze.

In early May I have a welcome surprise: The new foal has arrived. The mare is very skittish, wary of letting anyone too close to her new baby. This is a normal reaction for new mothers, and I have noticed it many times after the mares have foaled. I sit down and hope this makes me less of a threat. The mare, yearling, and new foal come trotting toward me to investigate. They are very curious. The Spanish stallion comes running from behind them and drives the inquisitive yearling away from me. I move so that the early morning sun is behind me, and the family approaches again, mare and yearling in the lead, and the little graying filly keeping up. The stallion nickers softly to the mare, head to head, very tender, and warns her to stay away from me, but then he approaches me himself. He walks to within 5 feet of me, but I am not concerned because his head is lowered, his posture is relaxed, his eye soft. He pauses a moment, then moves back behind his family and lets them move a little closer to me.

▲ *Rumbling softly and touching noses, the stallion reassures his mare and yearling*

THE BLACK STALLION

On a ridge overlooking the big meadow, there is a sudden flurry of activity. A white horse runs toward another stallion's band. Suddenly, two stallions are reaching for the sky, striking out and hitting each other with flying hooves. They fall back to earth then rear up again, black and white together. I wonder who will win. . . then the black stallion chases the white over the hill.

The wind is blowing so hard that I am forced to spread my legs to brace myself against its power. I slowly move closer to the black stallion's band. As soon as he senses my presence, the whole band wheels and turns away from me, running across the meadow, manes and tails streaming.

The next day, the black stallion's band is in the middle of the meadow surrounded by other bands of the Adobe Town Herd. I count more than 35 horses in the meadow and decide to walk slowly into the middle. The Spanish stallion's band is on my right, and the black stallion's band is on my left. Since the black stallion had been so skittish the day before, I circle around his band and wait to get closer until his attention is caught by another band's stallion. The black stallion's band includes a stocky chestnut colt, who stands very still next to his flashy, dappled-gray mother.

68

When the colt moves away from his mother, another mare, a very dark bay, who seems to act as a fond auntie to the colt, nuzzles him, apparently looking out for him in his mother's absence. Another member of the black stallion's band is a very dirty, delicate bay filly, who seems very shy.

When the black stallion finally notices my presence, he freezes, eyeing me. His long, matted mane blows gently away from his body, and I notice how big his feet are; he resembles draft-horse crosses I have seen, with thick feathers on his fetlocks and a large, solid body. Since he has only a couple of marks on his hide, he is most likely middle-aged. He starts trotting, and the mares, foal, and filly follow him, creating a running carousel around me. When the mares and foal get too close, the black stallion stops and snorts loudly, startling me. He drives them away from me, and then he relaxes and starts grazing.

On my next trip in June, I see the black stallion's band headed toward a creek under an old wooden bridge. Since it had recently rained, the water is up a few inches in what is usually a dry and sandy river bed. With purpose in their strides, the stallion in the rear, they move into the water, first drinking briefly. Their numbers have dwindled—the foal is gone, which surprises me since he was such a sturdy and healthy looking little youngster, and the dark gray mare is also gone. The light dappled-gray

mare leads the way–drinking, then pausing. She wanders a bit down stream, and the stallion calls to her, reminding her to cross the river and stay with him. Finally, they emerge from the stream and run playfully up the hill, outlined by the slanting rays of the late afternoon sun.

In July the temperature climbs into the high 90s, and horses move together, taking advantage of each other's tails as a fly whisks. One afternoon the clouds were gathering quickly, and I could see lightning in the distance. The black stallion and his band were standing head to tail until a sorrel stallion began moving into his territory.

From my first visit to Adobe Town, I periodically noticed huge piles of horse droppings along the road, which had made me curious until I observed a uniquely stallion behavior: As a stallion passes his piles, he adds to them. He is marking his territory.

As the sorrel stallion gets closer, the black stallion adds to a pile then makes the flehmen gesture, lifting his lip. The sorrel stallion comes running up to confront the black, and the two arch their necks, paw the ground, touch noses, and then break away, squealing. The black stallion chases the sorrel away from his band just as the lightning strikes very close to us, and the rain begins to pour. I run to my car, determined to leave before the roads turn into a sticky, slick trap for my vehicle. On the way back to town, as I skid across the mud, I see a band of horses picking their way through the torrents. They finally stop, waiting for the downpour to be over. I brake on the road just 7 feet from a big-headed chestnut stallion with rain cascading down his body. We keep each other company until the last of the rain passes, and he moves on with his band.

The next morning, after the road has dried, I find the black stallion's band grazing along the entrance to horse territory. I move slowly and indirectly out to them until I am about 25 feet away. Then I sit down to watch. The gray mare and the bay filly seem interested in me today, and they slowly approach. The black stallion trots toward me and stops. I finally get up and start moving toward my vehicle when I notice that the gray mare and bay filly have followed me. I stop, and they come within about 5 feet of me, just looking. The stallion watches but does not interfere. Finally they rejoin him, and I head on alone.

▲ *Because of holes in the fence, some bands trespass into the cattle allotment areas, and the ranchers push the BLM to schedule a roundup.*

THE RED ROAN STALLION

As I drive up a winding road, I see a group of horses at the top of a hill. I turn off the main road onto a rutted overgrown two-track to get closer. A red roan stallion with a dusting of white hairs and scars speckling his coat jerks his head up as my car stops, and when I open the door, he snorts and spins, running toward his band. A lovely red roan mare who looks like the stallion is in the front, and behind her is a black mare with a thick, dreadlocked mane and a black foal at her side. I crouch down, camera in hand, and wait to see what they will do about me. The stallion slowly approaches, coming about 10 feet away before he stops, but the mares, especially the beautiful black who is protective of her black colt, keep running up the hill. The stallion follows, looking over his shoulder a couple of times to make sure I am not following them.

The next time I see the red roan stallion, his family is reduced in size. The red roan mare is missing, which confirms to me that she is indeed his daughter. (In wild horse bands, when the fillies reach maturity, they usually wander off or are taken by rival stallions; it's nature's way of preventing inbreeding.) Their group is near the road in the first pasture that I pass as I enter the horse area. I wonder how they will handle my presence this time. The stallion tolerates my cautious approach, and the mare and colt look at me as if they wonder what type of creature I am. I ease into a sitting position, and they come closer still–I almost hold my breath–and then the stallion walks between me and them, as if to say, "This far, no further."

My next trip comes in wintertime. I spot the red roan across the road from his mare and colt. I almost do not recognize him because in winter, his white speckled coat has become a rich sorrel color. But there is no mistaking his distinctive long blaze, or that mare with her dazzling wild mane. Snow is falling heavily, and sound is muffled in the cold air. I approach the mare and colt, and the stallion runs to catch up with them, concerned by this possible threat to his family until he comes close enough to see and smell me. Then the band relaxes, and they settle down to the arduous task of finding grass under the deep snow.

82

The next day the sun comes out, and I see the red roan and his family once more close to the road. I slowly draw near them again, and take a seat on a mound of new grass. The black colt and his mother watch me for a while, then gradually edge nearer to me. I hear the crunch of snow on my left, and realize that the red roan stallion has come around behind me, and is only about 5 feet away! I hold my breath as he comes closer and closer. Well aware that he could hurt me if he chose, I stay very still, trusting his gentle nature. He walks all the way around me, then settles down to paw the snow in a search for grass.

Shortly before the Adobe Town roundup the following summer, I travel out to the horse area, and am delighted to find the red roan and his family still together. A new colt has been born this summer, and I am sure he is going to look like his daddy: The baby is shedding his foal coat already, and the new hair looks patchy and speckled. His older brother, the black colt, is going through that awkward leggy stage common in long yearlings, but still plays like a youngster with the foal. An adventurous fellow, the baby spends most of his time with his older brother or dad, only returning to mom long enough to nurse, and he only reluctantly surrenders to sleep.

ROUNDUP

OF THE ADOBE TOWN HERD

In the summer of 2005, I found out that the Bureau of Land Management was planning to bring the population of the Adobe Town Herd down to approximately 600-650 horses by utilizing a helicopter roundup. To maintain the Appropriate Management Levels (AMLs) for the wild horses in each area, the BLM hires contractors to gather the "excess" wild horses, most commonly by helicopter. The Adobe Town Herd Management Area consists of over 450,000 acres–which seems certainly large enough to accommodate the existing thriving and genetically viable 1200 horses. Nonetheless, the herd's BLM-assigned AML is much smaller, about 700 wild horses. Birth control is not an expensive or difficult way of managing herd size, yet the BLM opts not to utilize this method to maintain the population of the Adobe Town Herd. Instead, it continues to round up the horses in a procedure that is incredibly costly as well as stressful and traumatic for the horses themselves.

I observed the 2005 roundup for 4 days. The contractor was Cattoor, which is one of the original companies hired to round up wild horses and which still holds the majority of BLM contracts for gathers. They started in 1969 using riders on horses instead of helicopters, but now they maintain that roundups using helicopters are more humane since they are a much quicker method; the horseback gathers could take days of running and pursuing the horses before they could be captured. The helicopter is flown out to find a group of wild horses and then drives them to the trap area, which has camouflaged fencing that funnels into pens with gates that can be closed behind the horses. The horses are driven over rough country, over many miles–in the case of one large group, over 15 miles, an enormous and potentially debilitating distance for a horse to run at top speed. As the horses approach the trap, another horse is released, the "Judas" horse which has been trained to run into the trap, and the wild horses follow. The helicopter flies in close, confining the horses until the gate can be closed. Clouds of blinding dust are kicked up, and the noise is deafening.

The second day of the round-up, I recognized one of the bands from the Adobe Town Herd that I was hoping not to see. The red roan stallion was approaching, with his black mare, black yearling, and roan foal, all running within a huge group of horses. This was the small band I had often seen near the road, and the stallion which once grazed comfortably within a few feet of me.

The first thing that happens to the trapped and terrified horses is that they are separated from the rest of their band and then sorted by sex and age. The contractors drive the horses into a single-file line using "flags" (a plastic bag attached to the end of a stick), which scare the horses into moving.

Then each horse is pushed into a squeeze chute where it is held securely while its sex and age (by the appearance of its teeth) are determined. The mares are also checked to see if they are nursing. (The contractors call this being "wet.") At this roundup, the mares were separated from almost all the foals no matter how young the babies were. Wild foals should not be weaned earlier than six months; younger foals still need their mother's milk and can die without it. I found out later that 16 foals separated from their mothers were three months old or younger and had to be fostered out to people willing to bottle-feed them.

The horses are marked with paint on their rear ends as they pass through the chute: an X for release or a number for those that will be shipped to the Rock Springs facility for additional processing. There is a huge pen for the mares, another large pen for the stallions, and a smaller pen for foals and for a few mares with foals.

The horses most likely to be adopted are the youngsters and the younger adults. At this round-up, the contractor separated out the youngest and the oldest, and, in the sorting process, marked the stallions and mares over 5 or 6 years old for release. Other criteria were used as the sorting process went on: Those horses of unusual and desirable color such as blacks or roans are marked for release in hopes that they will breed others with these colors.

The red roan stallion, ears back, is angry at being forced into close proximity with other larger stallions ◀

At the beginning of this particular sorting, the older stallions, those over 10 years old and therefore subject to the Burns Sale Authority, were targeted for release; they would be allowed to live out their lives in freedom. However, halfway through the roundup the BLM representative reported that he had got 100 spots for stallions in the BLM long-term holding "sanctuaries" in Oklahoma, and so they would re-sort the stallions accordingly.

I was aghast. Why would the BLM prefer to further traumatize these aged horses when they wouldn't ever be offered for adoption and when the cost of their removal, transportation, and upkeep at these holding facilities is so high? And why take the older stallions? Almost all of them, ranging from 11 to 26 years old, were in healthy shape and deserved to live out their days unmolested instead of having to go through the trauma of being shipped to Rock Springs, castrated (which does kill a percentage of the horses), and then shipped to Oklahoma, a climate and landscape utterly different from any they had ever known.

Just what is this Burns Sale Authority, that allows the BLM to make this call? What happened to the original intent of the 1971 Congressional act? The answers lie in the politics of land management.

In November 2004, days before the Thanksgiving recess of Congress and the expiration of the current appropriations, Senator Conrad Burns from Montana introduced a rider to the Appropriations Bill with no opportunity for a public hearing or appeal. The Burns Amendment thus silently passed into law in December 2004. The Amendment provides what has become known as the Burns Sales Authority, which gives the Bureau of Land Management the authority to sell "excess" wild horses and burros without limitation, meaning they can be sold at auction for as little as a $1 per head. These horses seem likely to end up being slaughtered for meat. The Amendment that created the Authority defines "excess animals" as either those over 10 years of age or those that have been offered unsuccessfully for adoption at least three times. It further mandates the sale of the "excess animals" without limitation "until such time as all the excess animals offered for sale are sold; or the appropriate management level…is attained in all areas occupied by wild horses and burros."

As the contractor and crew sorted the horses, the red roan stallion, small but mighty, whom I had so often spent time with, was sent through the chute, and even as I was hoping for his release, they announced that he was 22 years old and loaded him into the big trailer for shipment to Oklahoma.

A chestnut stallion and gray mare came in together during the middle of the day. They stuck close together until they were separated, and once the mare was put in with the young mares and foals, she looked lost and kept calling for the stallion. The

BLM representative told me that she was blind. How amazing that she had adapted to living in an environment with uneven terrain and was able to be healthy and thriving in the company of her stallion. Yet now she was going to be put down because she would not be able to be adopted. I wondered why they didn't just release her and the stallion and allow her to live out her life with him.

I watched much of the round-up from a perch high on a huge rock formation over-looking the valley where the horses were driven down to the pens. About 100 yards from the entrance to the trap, I saw a young mare lie down. Then she struggled to get up, walked a few more steps, and went down again. Soon after the rest of the horses with her group had been secured, one of the wranglers rode out on his horse to get her. He roped her and pulled her up. She moved a few steps and then went down again. It was obvious that something was terribly wrong. Using a cattle prod the wrangler got her up time and again, and another wrangler joined him to help. They finally pulled her into the paneled area, where she lay down for the last time and finally died. Stress, colic, heart attack, or whatever, it was unclear exactly why she died, but it was a grim reminder of how stressful the whole process is for the horses, being driven by a deafening helicopter for miles without relief.

The contractors fed and watered the horses each day. I used these opportunities to go near the pens, since any approach was a major disruption; the horses would all move back quickly from the fence at any human approach, panicking and hitting

each other and the panels in a terrified attempt to get as far away as possible. The stallions had some fights while I watched, more scuffles than full blown battles, and many had fresh cuts and kicks and bites from the stress of being kept so close to other territorial males. One huge bay stallion's eye was almost closed from swelling, a new injury since he entered the pens. Most of the time, though, their fight was gone. Their heads hung down, in a weary, resigned manner. Looking into those eyes was one of the saddest things I have ever done.

Some of the horses were in the pens for up to a week before they were released because their disposition was in question and the contractor didn't want to have to round up the same horses all over again. They released the mares on one day to give them a chance to settle in, and then released the stallions the next day. I wondered how the stallions would find their mares, some of which had been with them for over a decade. I thought about the black stallion and his mare, a devoted pair I had seen almost every time I went out. They would probably never see each other again.

But seeing the 70 middle-aged stallions released was like an answer to a prayer—all that beautiful energy and joy to be free, the running, plunging, and all-out chaos as they sought to get as far from the hated pens as possible.

THE BLM HOLDING FACILITY

AT ROCK SPRINGS, WYOMING

Four weeks after the roundup I went to Rock Springs, Wyoming, to the BLM holding facility where the horses are processed through the system. They are tested for Equine Infectious Anemia, given vaccinations, and freeze-branded with a number. In addition, the stallions are castrated.

By the time I arrived, most of the older horses had already been shipped to the government-funded long-term holding areas in Kansas and Oklahoma. Some of the younger horses had been sent to Riverton Honor Farm in Wyoming to the prison training program or to private trainer Steve Mantle where the horses are gentled for 30 days before being offered for adoption. Once the horses are trained and sent to the Rock Springs holding facility, they may become eligible for adoption in a week. The previous adoption held at Rock Springs was not well attended, and the BLM were hoping for more people this time. The horses that are not adopted from Rock Springs would be shipped all over the country to different adoption facilities. If they are not adopted after three tries, they are then subject to sale through the Burns Sale Authority.

The Rock Springs facility, which can hold almost 700 horses, has pens with horses grouped by age and sex. As I walked around, I saw two dead horses lying on the ground in two different pens. The BLM representative who was giving me the tour was surprised and horrified, and begged me not to take a photograph.

When I returned to the facility's office, I inquired about the red roan stallion, since he was reported to have been shipped to Oklahoma. From the description of his markings, we determined his brand number, checked to make sure he wasn't one of the horses who died in the castration process, and found that he had already been shipped. I got the phone number of one of the long-term holding facilities in Oklahoma.

110

THE HUGHES RANCH

HOLDING FACILITY IN OKLAHOMA

A few weeks later, I arrived in Oklahoma at the Hughes Ranch, which maintains a long-term holding area that is home to 2000 gathered wild horses. The owner, John Hughes, told me he was one of the first ranchers to have a contract with the BLM to keep the wild horses, which he'd been doing since 1989. His ranch had been in his family for a long time, and they used to run cattle, but since winning the contract with the BLM, he has doubtless found that keeping the horses is more lucrative. Ironically, cattle ranching is notorious for being a difficult business to conduct profitably, and, clearly, the profits from keeping wild horses for the government at a guaranteed rate each year are higher than from grazing cattle. He told me that the horses are lighter on the land than the cattle and consumed less grass; thus, he could keep more of them on the same acreage. On thousands of acres of lush grass, these older horses live out their lives—for now. But a long-term facility such as the Hughes operation costs the BLM $1.25 per horse per day, and there are several such places in Oklahoma and Kansas.

112

I didn't see my old friend, the red roan, because he had been shipped to another ranch in Oklahoma, but the horses from Adobe Town that had come in the week before were in a smaller pasture so that they could get used to their new home. I sat down to watch them and observed that they ran just like wild horses out on the range and then settled down to graze. A pair did mutual grooming. These old former stallions (now geldings) included a black with a wide white blaze shaped like a rocket that was almost identical to the markings on the striking black stallion that is—I fervently hope—still running free in the Red Desert in Wyoming.

It may seem like an ideal life for these older horses, but because of the Burns Sale Authority, they can be sold at any time. When John Hughes was giving me a tour, he pointed out a stack of BLM corral panels of the same type used in the wild horse roundups. Apparently, shortly after the Burns Amendment passed in 2004, BLM representatives came out to the ranch and informed Hughes that they might soon be rounding up some of the horses to be sold under the Burns Sale Authority. They have not as yet done this. At some point, however, it seems inevitable that the cost for keeping these old horses is going to lead the BLM to sell them, in which case they most likely will end up at slaughterhouses. But, for now, the corral panels continue to lie rusting in the tall grass, a reminder of the fragile status of these formerly wild horses.

The older horses that have just arrived from Rock Springs stay in pens until they have gotten used to the fences and the ranch, and then they are released into huge pastures.

ADOBE TOWN AFTER THE ROUNDUP

After the removal of more than 800 horses from the Adobe Town Herd Area, the next roundup was scheduled for 2008. The BLM estimated that there were approximately 600 horses left in the herd area in September 2005. However, in the spring of 2006 the BLM posted their intent to do yet another roundup, only 1 ½ years later on the already traumatized and fragmented herd. An astonishing increase in the numbers of horses was cited as the reasoning. After a horse count in April 2006, the BLM combined the two adjoining horse areas, Adobe Town and Salt Wells, into a Complex, on the premise that the horses did not respect boundaries and moved freely between the two areas. In this count, using a small plane flying over the areas, the BLM counted 1500 horses between the two areas. This was substantially more than the estimated 900 after the roundup of fall 2005. However, in December of 2006, the BLM conducted yet another aerial survey and reported that there were 2200 horses between the two herd areas! Where did the extra 700 horses come from? Apparently, the BLM had used a statistical model for estimating horse numbers, and relying on that model, they proposed to remove 900 horses from Salt Wells and 800 from Adobe Town.

This roundup was scheduled for January of 2007, the very harshest month of the year, with temperatures often below zero, with freezing winds and snow drifts. Despite an outcry from the public about the possibility of sick and injured horses from severe weather conditions, the BLM removed more than 900 horses from Salt Wells. The only thing that prevented a subsequent removal from Adobe Town were the five foot snow drifts in the area. Perhaps the other factor, which of course the BLM did not mention, was that there were not 800 horses left in Adobe Town, because the actual numbers of horses in the area were, in fact, much lower than the inflated estimate from the statistical model.

Certainly, my experience upon visiting the area in April of 2007 showed me there were very few horses left. I was able to find 5 bands in areas that used to support 15 or more. The only familiar horse I encountered was the beautiful young black stallion, which I had seen so often before the roundup, and which had always been inseparable from his elegant black mare. I had seen that remarkable family driven in by helicopter, and thought then (and still do now) how very sad for such a tight band to be separated from each other forever. The stallion had been released, and that spring it was bittersweet to see him with his new family, two awkward yearlings who were playing and grooming each other.

I also spent time with a band that I thought I recognized from a distance, but upon a closer look, found it was not after all the familiar gray stallion's band. But surely this scarred gray stallion was a descendant of that other gray. This one was very protective of his family. His old white mare was almost crippled, with 2 large knees, and so the band traveled slowly to accommodate her. The yearling colt kept demanding attention from the stallion, opening and closing his mouth in that submissive behavior that the very young use to disarm older horses. The tolerant stallion groomed the youngster. When another band ran by them, they stood quietly, and watched them, then returned to the important business of grazing.

◄ *The yearling approaches the stallion opening and closing his mouth submissively*

▶ *The young black stallion and*

his original family, the black mare and foal.

▶ *The young black stallion's new family –*
a young mare and colt

WILD HORSE MISMANAGEMENT

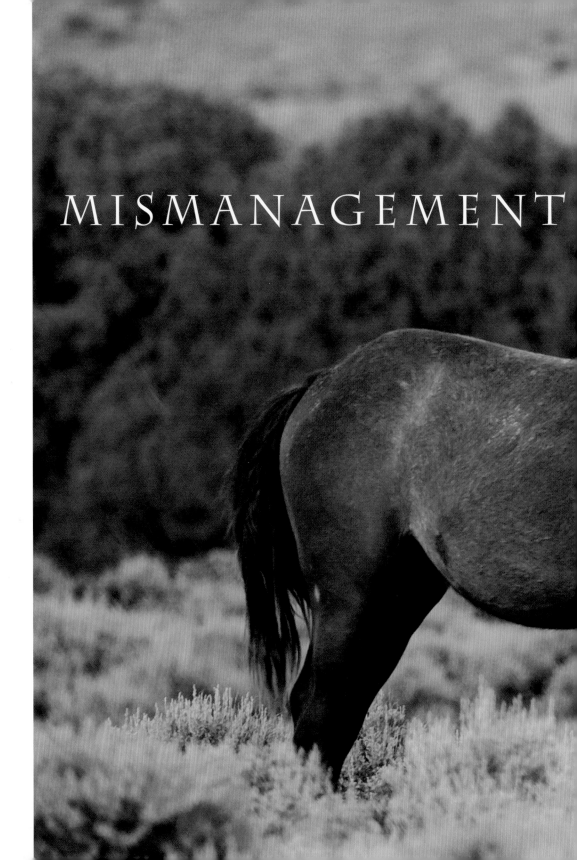

The fate of the Adobe Town Herd is not unique. Presently, most of the wild horses in this country are on public lands, administered by the Bureau of Land Management. The BLM public lands are just that: They belong to the public and are paid for by the taxpayers of the United States. The BLM must care for these lands, a task complicated by many competing interests.

The BLM is also responsible for issuing grazing permits to cattle ranchers, who lease areas of public lands at a very low rate–currently $1.35 per cow-calf pair per month, while the going rate on private land is $13 per pair per month. To a rancher, every wild horse represents competition for bargain-rate grazing land, while to public lands management, horses represent cost and cattle (and sheep) represent revenue. Currently, BLM public lands support approximately 200 head of cattle for

every one wild horse. Yet, with over 4 million cattle and over 6 million large game animals (elk, antelope, and deer) estimated to be on public lands and with only 24,000 wild horses left in the wild, the horses make up less than ½ of 1 percent of the large animals that are grazing on public land. In reality, removal of the wild horses, therefore, would make little impact even on overgrazed areas.

The BLM explains that they must keep numbers of wild horses low because they destroy the rangeland and because they reproduce at a very high rate, about 20-25% per year. The argument is that they will overpopulate areas and inevitably eat themselves to starvation. In 1982, a National Academy of Sciences report and two General Accounting Office reports found that horses reproduce at a much lower rate than the BLM contends, actually at only about 10% per year. The 1971 Wild Horse and Burro Act states that in a given area there is a certain amount of forage, and then when that amount is decreased by a certain percentage, there are deemed to be too many animals in that area. Cattle and sheep have been overwhelmingly favored over wild horses when selecting what appropriate numbers and types of animals are allowed in any given area, and wild horses have again and again been targeted for removal from public lands–this despite proof shown in many studies that the livestock grazers and not the wild horses are the main contributors to the

degradation of the land, soil erosion and loss of vegetation. Wild horses actually enhance their environment because their digestive systems don't completely break down seeds, and so their manure can be a source of germinating grass seeds after a fire or drought.

303 Herd Management Areas (HMAs) were originally designated for wild horses. All of the wild horses have now been removed from 102 of them. In the remaining 201 areas, the BLM has assigned Appropriate Management Levels, or "AMLs," that for the most part consist of very low numbers of wild horses. Low numbers of horses in a herd area threatens the genetic viability of the herds, according to Dr. Gus Kothren, director of the Equine Blood Types Research Laboratory at Texas A&M. Based on his studies of the Pryor Mountain Herd in Montana, Dr. Kothren maintains that the wild horse herds should consist of between 150 and 200 horses in order to ensure genetic viability and to prevent inbreeding. In light of these findings, the wild horse populations in 75% of the remaining Herd Management Areas are in danger of extinction if managed at the current AML levels. Some of these Herd Management Areas are vast, hundreds of thousands of acres in size, yet they have AMLs of only 50-100 horses per area. Some glaring examples are the Little Colorado HMA in Wyoming with ½ million acres and an AML of only 100 horses, and the Spring Mountain HMA in Nevada with 575,000 acres and an AML of only 50 horses. It is hard to understand the logic behind this incongruity without concluding that wild horses are being managed to extinction.

In some areas, such as in the Pryor Mountains in Montana, where the BLM has been accused of planning to reduce the herd below the level of genetic viability, the agency has answered by suggesting that they import horses from another herd. But this would result in the loss of the unique characteristics of the Pryor Mountain herd. At least four of the herds on public land (the Pryor Mountain herd in Montana, the Cerbat herd in Arizona, the Kiger herd in Oregon, and the Sulfur herd in Utah) have all been tested and found to have Spanish ancestry and have strong Spanish links. These herds should be managed for their unique characteristics and allowed to recover to genetically viable levels.

Above: Sheep share the Adobe Town herd area with the horses in early spring. Cattle graze there in spring and summer.

At right: In the last three years, exploration and drilling for oil and gas have increased exponentially in the Adobe Town herd area, and in many other wild horse areas. In some of those areas, the wild horses are being squeezed out, despite the fact that they do not compete with the oil and gas interests for resources.

Removing one horse from the range costs $3100, on top of which there is the cost for the long-term maintenance of each horse that is not adopted. The net result of the current BLM removal program is a bill to taxpayers of $39 million per year. The BLM admits that its adopter program numbers were down to about 5100 in 2006, yet they rounded up more than 10,000 wild horses that year. In 2007, more than 7000 horses were removed, and the proposed roundup schedule for 2008 targets 6000 or more for removal.

Where should all these animals go? Arguably, many go to caring homes and wise horsemen and women. Unfortunately, though, not every person can provide a good home for a wild horse; these horses, especially in the early days after they are adopted, frequently need special care and knowledgeable handling. When their adopted homes fail to work out, these horses are often destined for slaughter.

After caring for an adopted wild horse for 1 year, an adopter receives title or ownership from the Federal Government under the current wild horse adoption program. More than 207,000 wild horses and burros were placed by the BLM between 1973 and 2005. The minimum adoption fee is $125, and there are requirements that must be met to become an adopter. The program appears to have safeguards protecting the horses; to believe these protections are iron-clad is to be naïve about the political process.

One only needs to remember that under the Burns Sale Authority, some wild horses can be sold for as little as $1 and there is no waiting period for receiving title to the horse. In April of 2005, 41 wild horses sold under the Burns Sales Authority were slaughtered for meat. After the public outcry, the BLM temporarily suspended sales of the horses, but then resumed sales in late May 2005. As a result, in the first year the Burns Sales Authority was in effect, over 1500 horses were sold.

In February of 2006 the BLM announced a new program encouraging cattle ranchers to purchase wild horses from the stock of 8000 eligible to be sold, at the bargain price of $10 per head, in order to free up holding space so that more horses could be rounded up and removed from public lands. Given that the cattle ranchers are the people who have been pushing the hardest to remove horses from public lands, this seems a clear invitation to market the horses for slaughter, which the buyers may legally do once they receive title to the horses.

Yet another threat to wild horses is a new proposal called "Instant Titling." The BLM is currently in discussion about this with the National Wild Horse and Burro Advisory Board. This proposal would allow all adopters (not only buyers under the Burns Authority) to receive ownership title to any wild horse immediately upon adoption, removing any protection of the wild horses from sale for slaughter.

Another drastic and ill-conceived plan that the BLM is proposing is the use of sterilization to control the population in 49 herd areas, including Adobe Town. Under this plan, 25% of the stallions in these designated areas would be rounded up, then castrated and returned to the herds. The trauma and stress to these stallions subjected to the castration process and removal from their families would be immense.

136

The older blue roan stallion suddenly wakes up from his midmorning nap, and checks his bay mare's readiness for breeding. He attempts to mount her despite her obvious reluctance. After a strong kick, he subsides and begins to graze as if nothing happened.

The band of three mares is unique in my experiences with wild horses. The oldest mare, probably the mother of the two younger mares, acts just like a stallion, snaking her neck at the other two and driving them around aggressively. She was even scarred from bites just like the stallions.

SOLUTIONS FOR THE FUTURE

The simplest solution for the wild horses would be to raise the allotment numbers to allow genetically viable numbers of horses to remain in the BLM's Herd Management Areas. With intense pressure from cattle ranchers, oil and gas drillers, and other interests, wild horse AMLs have been on the decrease, even in areas where vast acreage and adequate forage render the AMLs ridiculously low. One solution is for the BLM to pay the cattle ranchers who hold grazing allotments a per-horse fee to allow the horses to stay on the ranchers' leased public lands area. This would give the rancher some compensation for decreased grazing land and it would help the horses by eliminating the stress of the roundup and the trauma of being separated from their bands. It would also eliminate the high cost to the taxpayer of shipping horses across the country, and feeding and housing them in long-term holding areas.

142

Wilderness areas should be provided for the use of the wild horses. In these areas, where there is enough range to support the horses over the long term, nature should be allowed to regulate their numbers. Predators such as mountain lions would be an important part of controlling the wild horse population. Studies could be conducted in areas like these to investigate whether or not the wild horse can regulate its numbers with enough land and the right conditions and maintain a genetically viable population without outside interference.

Horses evolved in North America thousands of years ago and were believed to have crossed to Asia over the Bering Land Bridge that connected Alaska to Siberia over 8000 years ago. Speculation over the cause of their extinction on this continent ranges from a climate change that caused them to die out or to migrate, to hunting by early man. If evidence were found to prove that not all the horses had died out in North America, the wild horse could be extended protection as a native species and even allowed into National Parks instead of persecuted as a "feral" animal. However, researchers who are currently analyzing the mitochondrial DNA of horses have demonstrated that the horse evolved in North America as a native species and was reintroduced by the Spanish in 1500s.

Pharmaceutical (rather than surgical) fertility control has been and continues to be used with mixed results. On the one hand, it is less invasive and less expensive than roundups. A 2004 study by the U.S. Geologic Survey reports that the BLM could

144

save $7.7 million dollars by using contraceptive measures. Porcine Zone Pellucida (PZP) has been used in the Pryor Mountain Herd in Montana. It is important to keep in mind that the numbers of wild horses need to be maintained at a certain level even in the herds where fertility control is used. Some issues have emerged that recommend caution when viewing the use of PZP as the best answer to maintaining appropriate herd sizes. For example, there is some evidence that it might lead to the total sterilization of young female horses and to the birth of out-of-season foals, which jeopardizes the health of both mares and their foals.

Private wild horse sanctuaries are on the increase, giving refuge to excess wild horses and allowing them to live out their lives without the threat of ending up at a slaughterhouse. There is a need for more of these sanctuaries, because the fate of wild horses on public lands is constantly subject to changes in legislation. Funding is always an issue, of course. Some private sanctuaries have used the idea of having people "sponsor" individual, named horses to help pay for the expense of maintaining them. They also hold fundraisers to support the cost of maintaining the horses.

Tourism with wild horses as the focus is a very important idea to be explored and developed. Wild horse tours could allow the horses on public lands to be perceived as having monetary value instead of being dismissed as monetary drain. Wild horses live in some of the most inaccessible areas, but tour operators who invest in developing this kind of opportunity would not only create good public relations for the horses, they would bring a welcome infusion of tourist dollars to boost local and state economies.

▶ *A stallion and mare engaged in mutual grooming, a common activity for domestic and wild horses.*

People in this country love these horses–we are in awe of their grace and wildness, and enjoy their freedom as symbolic of our own. Would people not pay to see them in their natural habitat, which is, after all, on our public lands? I believe they would. I believe horse lovers, wildlife enthusiasts, and Western history enthusiasts should be able to observe wild horse behavior under natural conditions and enjoy the opportunity to experience an important part of our country's unique Western heritage.

Legislation is extremely important to the cause of the wild horses. Until recently, there were three slaughterhouses in the United States used to process approximately 100,800 horses per year. In addition, as many as 30,000 horses were annually shipped to slaughterhouses in Canada and Mexico, with the meat typically making its way to Europe and Asia for human consumption. Currently, all three of the U.S. slaughterhouses have been closed down due to Federal Court rulings, but horses are still being transported to Mexican and Canadian slaughterhouses, now at a furious rate. The American Horse Slaughter Prevention Act, which passed last year overwhelmingly in the House of Representatives as H.R. 249 is currently stalled in the Energy and Natural Resource Committee in the Senate. If passed, this act will close this back door to slaughter and force the BLM to find other solutions for managing the wild horses on public land.

Once protection is restored to the wild horses, Congress should review the current wild horse management policies and recommend much needed changes. Public opinion will always be the most powerful tool for effecting change in Congress, and it is essential that people who care about the fate of the wild horses speak out for change. The American Wild Horse Preservation Campaign, at www.wildhorse-preservation.com, is an important resource with information about current issues facing the horses; this site also includes an online petition that you can sign.

The wild horses of America cannot speak for themselves, yet they are an unquestionable part of our national heritage. Since these horses are on our public lands, they "belong" to all Americans, so it is the American public that now needs to take action to save them. I hope that this book will help motivate you to fight for their survival. Our wild horses deserve to live free forever.

REFERENCES

American Wild Horse Preservation Campaign
www.wildhorsepreservation.com
Retrieved July 6, 2006.

Brungart, Kurt. "Galloping Scared." Vanity Fair, November 2006.

Bureau of Land Management Wild Horse and Burro Statistics
www.wildhorseandburro.blm.gov/statistics/index.htm
Retrieved October 31, 2006.

Bureau of Land Management Wild Horse and Burro Program
www.wildhorseandburro.blm.gov/index.php
Retrieved August 10, 2006.

Dobie, J. Frank. The Mustangs. Lincoln: University of Nebraska Press, 2005.

Downer, Craig. "Travesty of Justice." Sept. 22, 2004

American Wild Horse Preservation Campaign website
www.wildhorsepreservation.com/resources/downer.html
Retrieved October 30, 2006.

International Society for Protection of Mustangs and Burros
www.ispmb.org
Retrieved November 5, 2006.

Kirkpatrick, Jay F. Ph.D and Fazio, Patricia M. Ph.D.
"Wild Horses as Native American Wildlife."
March 2, 2005.

American Wild Horse Preservation Campaign website.
www.wildhorsepreservation.com/resources/native.html
Retrieved July 10, 2006.

Lococo, Andrea. "Fact, Fiction on West's Wild Horses."
The Denver Post, June 5, 2005.

Preston, Charles R. Buffalo Bill Historical Center, 2004.
Unbroken Spirit: The Wild Horse in the American Landscape.
www.bbhc.org/exhibitions/wildHorses.cfm
Retrieved November 17, 2006.

Ryden, Hope. America's Last Wild Mustangs.
Guilford: Lyons Press, 1999.

Stillman, Deanna. "Mustang Sallies: Can America's Wild Horses Survive
Another 4 Years of Bush?"
Washington Post Newsweek Interactive Co. LLC
http://slate.com/id/2113580
Retrieved November 15, 2006.

The Wild Free-Roaming Horse and Burro Act of 1971
(Public Law 92-195)
As amended by The Federal Land Policy and Management Act of 1976
(Public Law 94-579) and the Public Rangelands Improvement Act of 1978
(Public Law 95-514).
www.wilderness.net/NWPS/documents/publiclaws/PDF/92-195.pdf

Walker, Carol. "Wild Horses at Risk."
Practical Horseman, July 2005.

Wild Horses: An American Romance, PBS
http://net.unl.edu/artsFeat/wildhorses/
Retrieved November 4, 2006.

RESOURCES

This is not meant to be an exhaustive list of organizations dedicated to saving wild horses but is rather a list of places where you can go for information, education, and ideas on appropriate actions you can personally take to help ensure the survival of America's wild horses.

The American Wild Horse Preservation Campaign
www.wildhorsepreservation.com

The Cloud Foundation
www.thecloudfoundation.org

Humane Society of the United States
www.hsus.org

American Wild Horse Sanctuary (Return to Freedom)
www.returntofreedom.org

American Society for the Prevention of Cruelty to Animals
www.aspca.org

International Society for the Protection of Mustangs & Burros
www.ispmb.org

National Horse Protection Coalition
www.horse-protection.org

International Fund for Horses
www.fund4horses.org

ABOUT THE AUTHOR

Carol's passion for photography started at an early age, with animals as her favorite subjects. She studied literature and photography as an undergraduate at Smith College, and continued her education in photography after graduating, studying portraiture and nature photography. She has travelled all over the world photographing wildlife for the past 28 years.

In 2000, Carol started her business Living Images by Carol Walker, specializing in photographing horses. Carol's images illuminate the relationship between horses and their people, as well showcase the beauty of horses with her stunning images of horses at liberty. Her commercial work includes catalogue covers for leaders in the Equine industry. She has had numerous calendars published featuring her work, and she markets her fine art prints from her website www.LivingImagesCJW.com as well as in several locations on the Front Range of Colorado.

Four years ago, Carol began photographing wild horses. As she followed several herds in Wyoming, Colorado and Montana, she became aware of how precarious their situation on public lands has become. Since then, she has dedicated herself to educating people with her photographs and stories about the wild horses.

Author photo by Charles Hilton

Order Extra Copies of Wild Hoofbeats

Wild Hoofbeats Book – Only $29.95 US
Wild Hoofbeats Calendar – Only $11.95 US

Shipping & Handling for 1 book plus calendar,
or 1 book, or 1 calendar:

U.S. Standard – $5.00
U.S. Expedited – $12.00
Canada Standard – $12.00
Canada Expedited – $20.00
International Standard – $25.00
International Expedited – $35.00

Order Today! Either by mail with this form (a printable version of this order form for order by mail is also available on the website) or order online at www.WildHoofbeats.com. We accept MasterCard, VISA and American Express, PayPal, checks and money orders.

For more information about both the Wild Hoofbeats Book and Calendar, or to order online, please visit

www.WildHoofbeats.com

10% of all proceeds of the *Wild Hoofbeats* Book and Companion Calendar will go to the Cloud Foundation

THE CLOUD FOUNDATION

Dedicated to the preservation of wild horses on our public lands and the protection of Cloud's herd in the Arrowhead Mountains of Montana.

To learn more about The Cloud Foundation visit www.thecloudfoundation.org

YES! I want to order Wild Hoofbeats!

Name _____

Address _____

City _____

State _____ Zip _____

Wild Hoofbeats Book

          Qty _____ @ $29.95 US   SubTotal _____

Wild Hoofbeats
Companion Calendar   Qty _____ @ $11.95 US   SubTotal _____

Shipping & Handling: (see at left)   _____

                              Total Due _____

PAYMENT OPTIONS:

❏ **Send a check or money order by postal mail to:**
    Painted Hills Publishing
    16500 Dakota Ridge Road
    Longmont, CO 80503

Enclose a check or money order for the amount due made out to Painted Hills Publishing. Please note: Product will not be shipped until payment has been received.

Credit Card (check one) ❏ MasterCard ❏ VISA ❏ American Express

Card Number _____

Security Code _____   Exp. Date _____

Signature _____

Also Available! The 2009 Wild Hoofbeats Calendar

Over 70 stunning wild horse photos by Carol grace this handsome Wild Hoofbeats companion calendar, including favortites from the book Wild Hoofbeats as well as many new images not included in the book.

Only $11.95!
See Shipping & Handling costs at left

www.WildHoofbeats.com